A BOOK OF FEARS

by

LEWIS TURCO

translated into Italian by

JOSEPH ALESSIA

Preface by

FELIX STEFANILE

BORDIGHERA

Library of Congress Cataloging-in-Publication Data

Turco, Lewis.
   A book of fears / by Lewis Putnam Turco ; treanslated into Italian
by Joseph Alessia ; preface by Felix Stefanile.
       p.   cm. -- (Bordighera Poetry Prize ; 1)
   Poems in English and Italian.
   ISBN 1-884419-19-4 (alk. paper). -- ISBN 1-884419-20-8 (pbk. :
alk. paper)
   1. Turco, Lewis--Translations into Italian. I. Alessia, Joseph, 1937-
. II. Title. III. Series.
PS3570.U626B66   1998
811'.54—dc21   98-18976
                                                    CIP

Printed in the United States.

Published by
BORDIGHERA, INC.
Purdue University
1359 Stanley Coulter Hall
West Lafayette, IN 47907-1359

BORDIGHERA POETRY PRIZE 1
ISBN 1-884419-20-8 (softcover)
ISBN 1-884419-19-4 (hardcover)

OTHER BOOKS BY LEWIS TURCO

Shaking the Family Tree, 1998

Bordello: A Portfolio of Poemprints, with George O'Connell, 1996

How to Write a Miſſion, with A. Dibell and O. S. Card, 1995
(London)

Emily Dickinson, Woman of Letters, 1993

Il Dialogo, tr. Silvia Biasi, 1992 (Milan)

The Public Poet, Five Lectures on the Art and Craft of Poetry, 1991

The Shifting Web: New and Selected Poems, 1989

*Dialogue: A Socratic Dialogue on the Art of Writing Dialogue in
Fiction*, 1989

The Fog: A Chamber Opera in One Act, with Walter Hekster, 1987
(Amsterdam)

The New Book of Forms, 1986

A Maze of Monsters, 1986

Visions and Revisions of American Poetry, 1986

Poetry: An Introduction Through Writing, 1973

The Literature of New York: A Selective Bibliography, 1970

Awaken, Bells Falling: Poems 1959-1967, 1968

The Book of Forms: A Handbook of Poetics, 1968

First Poems, 1960

Dedicated to my
Artist collaborator
Of more than a quarter
Century, George O'Connell,
Who did this beautiful cover.
It's been a great pleasure,
George, and a great friendship.

ACKNOWLEDGMENTS

The author owes thanks and acknowledgment for original publication to *Abiko Quarterly* (Japan) for "Nomatophobia" and "Zelophobia"; *The American Literary Review* for "Ambiguphobia" and "Amnesiophobia"; *The Cream City Review* for "Parturiphobia"; *The Formalist* for "Ennuiophobia," Mnemophobia," and "Oneirophobia"; *The Hampden-Sydney Poetry Review* for "Quiescophobia"; *The New York Quarterly* for "Amathophobia," "Monophobia" and "Papyrophobia"; *The Southern Humanities Review* for "Arachnophobia"; *Wordsmith* for "Aelurophobia" and "Catoptrophobia," and to the *Scarecrow Poetry* anthology edited by Robert McGovern and Steven Haven, Ashland Poetry Press, 1994 for "Chronophobia" and "Gerascophobia."

PREFACE

Lewis Turco has earned his reputation not only as a poet, but as a scholar and a biographer. His books on poetry, its forms, and its prosody, are used in the schools. All of these gifts serve the poet in his latest collect, *A Book of Fears*. Mr. Turco's intellectual poise and stylistic grace are familiar to readers of poetry, but what makes this book a canny departure from his other work is the choice of personality types Mr. Turco presents to us. There is a touch of the psychological case study in Mr. Turco's offerings of "self portraits" this time.

The characters in *A Book of Fears* share, regardless of their varied lives, certain traits, moods and fears, certain preoccupations that mark them off from general society. What makes these lonely souls kin to each other is that they are all imprisoned by their obsessions, so that though they are distinct from each other as individuals, as far as the eye can see, they suffer the same disease, self-entrapment. Their hyperattentiveness to their flaws, like the man who studies his approaching baldness with the fervor of a DNA-biologist, is the telltale sign of a spiritual malaise that assails them all. This gives to the poet's tone an underlay of familiar motifs, as if Mr. Turco is singing to the same tune, but with different words.

My observation on this double thrust of difference with similarity is, of course, only partly true, but the *partliness* I am speaking of is essential to the construction of the poems, and give them their family resemblance. For instance, Mr. Turco patterns his syntax from character to character in such a way that often, sonically — and in terms of breath — the lyrics echo each other, and create a murmur that runs through the book. This is what I mean by underlay. Perhaps Mr. Turco will agree with me that often his syntax "rhymes" from page to page. In this manner the poet is telling us something about his art, as well as about the souls he is studying.

The gallery of portraits, of characters, is a traditional poetic mode, of ancient lineage. Mr. Turco has given us his contributions to this form in other books. *A Book of Fears* however, points to social criticism of a strictly contemporary kind in which his biographer's eye for detail fixes on the milieus of advertising, fad, and the headlines of today for his imagery and discourse. Ours is a society of name brands, sexual idiom, victimology as hobby and so on. His poet's skill brings art to this spiritual squalor not as a praise for such matters, but as a new theme for poets to ponder. In other words, he does what serious poets always manage to do: he takes topic, and makes it theme. How far you wish to take Mr. Turco's journey into the quibbling maelstrom of contemporary sensibility is your business, but in his honor, his chamber music of up-to-date speech rhythms, his scholarly patience with the trivia and tragedy of twentieth-century urban life in the United States, this guide will tell you things you didn't think you knew.

Felix Stefanile

TABLE OF CONTENTS

A BOOK OF FEARS

by

Lewis Turco

translated into Italian by

Joseph Alessia

CHOROPHOBIA
The Fear of Dancing

He watches the dancers skimming across the floor
holding one another, letting go,
falling away and coming together,
approaching and passing. "Come on, let's dance,"
she says. He shakes his head,

and as he does so the ballroom wobbles,
the dancers shift and shimmer
holding one another, letting go,
falling away and down because the floor
is a firmament of whirling dots of light —

he watches the dancers skimming across a floor
insubstantial as a summer sky.
The music murmurs among the whirling lights
like zephyrs beneath the stars, falling away,
approaching and passing. He shuts his eyes

because the floor is a firmament of shadow
deckled with dots of light spinning away.
The dancers shift and shimmer, begin to fall
through the spaces between the dots of light,
begin to fall holding one another.

COROFOBIA
La paura del ballo

Lui guarda i ballerini prillare nella pista
tenendosi l'uno all'altro, lasciandosi andare,
separandosi e riunendosi,
avvicinandosi ed allontanandosi. "Andiamo, balliamo,"
dice lei. Lui scuote la testa,

mentre la pista vacilla,
i ballerini si scambiano e luccicano
tenendosi l'uno all'altro, lasciandosi andare,
separandosi ed inchinandosi perchè la pista
è un firmamento turbinante di luccichii —

lui guarda i ballerini prillare nella pista
eterei come il cielo estivo.
La musica mormora tra le luci danzanti
come zeffiri sotto le stelle, separandosi,
avvicinandosi ed allontanandosi. Lui chiude gli occhi

perchè la pista è un firmamento di ombre
segnato da luccichii che si allontanano rapidamente.
I ballerini si scambiano e s'illuminano, vanno giù
negli spazi tra i luccichii,
vanno giù tenendosi l'uno all'altro.

MONOPHOBIA
The Fear of Loneliness

She sits by herself at a table, not the bar,
slowly stirring her warming cocktail, listening
to the buzz of conversation — the softball chat,
who dumped whom and when and why and where.
A cirrus of smoke is suspended in the air.

She smiles at him. He passes by. Another
takes his place. She smiles again and sips
her warming cocktail. "May I sit down?" he asks.
She nods, he sits. "Buy you a drink?" "Okay."
While he is gone she drinks her warming cocktail.

When he returns he says, "So, what's your name?
Mine's. . . ." She doesn't catch it. What's the difference,
anyway? But she tells him hers. They add
to the buzz of conversation — who knows whom
and where and when and why. But no one knows

any other, she thinks and does not think.
She stirs her warming cocktail now and then,
and when it's time to go she takes her bag
and follows him through the buzz of conversation,
the cirrus of smoke suspended in the air.

MONOFOBIA
La paura della solitudine

E' seduta ad un tavolo da sola, non al bar,
rimescola lentamente il suo cocktail che riscalda, ascoltando
il brusio della conversazione — i pettegolezzi di softball,
chi si è sbarazzato di chi e quando e perchè e dove.
Un cirro di fumo è sospeso nell'aria.

Lei gli sorride. Lui passa oltre. Un altro prende
il suo posto. Lei sorride di nuovo e centellina il suo
cocktail che riscalda. "Posso sedermi?" lui domanda.
Lei fa cenno col capo, lui si siede. "Posso offrirle da bere?" "Okay."
Mentre lui va al bar, lei beve il suo cocktail che riscalda.

Quando lui ritorna dice, "Bè, come ti chiami?
Il mio. . . ." Lei non capisce. Ma che differenza c'è?
Poi gli dice il nome. Si uniscono
al brusio della conversazione — chi conosce chi
e dove e quando e perchè. Ma nessuno conosce

altri, lei pensa e non pensa.
Lei rimescola di tanto in tanto il suo cocktail che riscalda,
e quando è ora di andare lei prende la borsa
e lo segue nel brusio della conversazione,
il cirro di fumo sospeso nell'aria.

QUIESCOPHOBIA
The Fear of Silence

On a line by John Gilgun

He awakens in the darkness hearing
nothing — does this silence
hold a secret at its center? There is
not a timber creaking nor the ticking
of a timepiece, only stillness

at the center of awareness,
only emptiness and shadow. He
turns on the light and listens — still
there's little in the quiet but his
breathing, so he holds his breath to listen

to the dancing of his nerve-ends, to the straining
of his throat, the tongue as dry as fever.
Can this silence hold the secret
at the center of the dance?
And the dance . . . the dance, what is it?

What's that noise? He startles — only stillness
rushing through his veins, the surge of blood
within his eardrums, in his arteries
the whirling of his hours, of his being
in the silence at the center of the dance.

QUIESCOFOBIA
La paura del silenzio

Su un verso di John Gilgun

Si sveglia nel buio senza sentir
nulla — questo silenzio
ha un segreto nel suo centro? Non si sente
nè il cigolio della legna, nè il ticchettio
dell'orologio, solamente solitudine

al centro della consapevolezza,
solo vuoto ed ombra. Lui
accende la luce ed ascolta — ma
si ode ben poco nel silenzio, tranne il suo
respiro, perciò lo mantiene per ascoltare

il formicolio sulla punta dei suoi nervi, lo sforzo
della gola, la lingua secca come la febbre.
Può questo silenzio avere il segreto
al centro del ballo?
E il ballo . . . il ballo, cos'è?

Cos'è quel rumore? Sussulta — sente solo solitudine
scorrere nelle vene, l'affluire del sangue
ai timpani, nelle arterie
il passare impetuoso delle ore, del suo essere
nel silenzio al centro del ballo.

PARTURIPHOBIA
The Fear of Childbirth

He's not for her, no matter who he is.
It's all his fault — the blood, the pain, the mess.
She's not responsible for the stocking of the planet —
let someone else do that. Too many people
anyway as it is. She looks at him

and shudders — the tremor begins about waist high
and travels down her hips, along her thighs,
ends at her knees. She feels her stomach turn
and looks away. He's not for her, no matter
what. She doesn't need the mess, the pain,

the blood, the squalling brat for the rest of her life.
She recalls her younger brother and what he did —
he's responsible for what happened to
their mother, he and her father — she's well out
of that; she'll never see either of them

the rest of her life. Let someone else do that,
go see the murderers in their jackals' lair.
She smooths her hair, looks up and sees another
coming in the door. She almost stares,
but he is not for her, never for her.

PARTURIFOBIA
La paura del parto

Lui non fa per lei, non importa chi sia.
E' tutta colpa sua — il sangue, il dolore, il caos.
Non è suo dovere ripopolare il pianeta —
lo facciano gli altri. Comunque
c'è già troppa gente. Lei lo guarda

e rabbrividisce — il tremore comincia dalla vite
e scende giù alle anche, lungo le cosce,
e si arresta alle ginocchia. Sente una stretta allo stomaco
e guarda altrove. Lui non fa per lei, non si discute.
Lei non si merita il caos, il dolore,

il sangue, il monello ribelle per tutta la sua vita.
Ricorda il fratello minore e le sue azioni —
è lui il responsabile di quanto è accaduto alla
mamma, lui e il padre — ma tutto
è passato per lei; non vedrà nessuno dei due

vita durante. Lo facciano gli altri,
che guardino gli assassini nel loro covo di sciacalli.
Lei si ravvia i capelli, alza gli occhi e vede un altro
che entra. Sta per fissarlo,
ma non fa per lei, mai più per lei.

PEDOPHOBIA
The Fear of Children

He sees them on the sidewalk before his doorway
and begins to sweat. What can he do? How
can he negotiate those laughing voices,
those whirling arms, the quizzing eyes, how
get into his apartment and be safe

behind the dusty windows closed against
the nasty games, the screams, the dirty faces?
He crosses the street and keeps on walking. He
goes slowly as he can around the block,
keeping watch against another clot

of children or a lone minute assassin.
When he approaches home again carrying his bag
of groceries he sees them still before his door.
He bites his lip. He walks quickly among
the laughing voices, whirling arms, dirty

faces, the screams, the staring eyes. He walks
stumbling up the stairs and through the door,
drops his burden on the couch, reaches
trembling for the shade, pulls it down
over the dusty panes, the life, the laughter.

PEDOFOBIA
La paura dei bambini

Li vede sul marciapiede davanti all'ingresso di casa
e suda freddo. Cosa fare? Come
conciliare quelle voci allegre,
quelle mani gesticolanti, gli occhi beffanti, come
entrare nel suo appartamento e sentirsi al sicuro

dietro le finestre polverose chiuse
ai giochi dispettosi, alle grida, ai visi sporchi?
Attraversa la strada e continua a camminare.
Gira molto lentamente intorno all'isolato,
tenendo d'occhio un'altra combriccola

di bambini o un solitario piccolo assassino.
Quando si ritrova davanti a casa con la borsa
della spesa, li vede ancora davanti alla porta.
Si morde le labbra. Accelera il passo tra
le voci allegre, le mani gesticolanti, i visi

sporchi, gli strilli, gli sguardi inquisitori. Avanza
inciampando sulle scale e sull'entrata,
depone il peso sul sofà, afferra
la tendina tremando, l'abbassa
sui vetri polverosi, sulla vita, sulle risa.

NOMATOPHOBIA
The Fear of Names

What shall she name it? She cannot bear to think —
Prudence, Penelope, Phyllis, Faith, Frenosia?
Oh, what will happen if she conjures up
a demon with these names? What if her child
turns out to be a monster? Beelzebub,

Old Ned himself, Scratch, Murgatroyd or Mabel —
Worms on the page that wriggle and writhe and wrine?
She cannot bear to think of what to name it:
Blister and Bore, Bumjohn, Barticle, Bruce,
Antichrist, Jesus! Bessy, Blossom, Livelong,

Love-in-a-Mist. Surely she must be mad —
Don't call her Shirley, Sherryl, Shunaboy, Suze,
what's in a name? A Rose by any other
anagram would be as Sore. She drops
the dictionary upon the floor. She weeps

and strikes her brow with the hardel of her hand:
Horace and Hosmer, Hokestraw, Wellington, Widge,
Trifosa after great grandma, Luigi, Drew. . . .
Knute the Unlucky, Erik the Dreadful, Alice,
Alas and Alack! What in the world will she do?

NOMATOFOBIA
La paura dei nomi

Come lo chiamerà? Non può sopportare di pensare —
Prudenza, Penelope, Fillide, Fede, Frenosia?
Oh, che succederà se evoca
un demonio con questi nomi? E se
suo figlio si rivelerà un mostro? Beelzebub,

il vecchio Ned in persona, Scretch, Murgatroyd o Mabel —
Vermi sulla pagina che si contorcono, si snodano, si flettono?
Non può sopportare di pensare come chiamarlo:
Blister e Bore, Bumjohn, Barticle, Bruce,
Anticristo, Gesù! Bessy, Blossom, Livelong,

Love-in-a-Mist. Sarà sicuramente arrabbiata —
Perchè non chiamarla Shirley, Sherryl, Shunaboy, Suze,
cosa c'è in un nome? "Anno" usando un altro
anagramma potrebbe diventare "nano." Butta
il dizionario sul pavimento. Piange

e si tocca la fronte con il carpo della mano:
Orazio e Hosmer, Okestraw, Wellington, Widge,
Trifosa come la bisnonna, Luigi, Drew. . . .
Knute lo Sfortunato, Erick il Terribile, Alice
Alas e Alack! Che diavolo farà mai?

APEIROPHOBIA
The Fear of Infinity

He lies awake in his bed
in the pit of night, gazing into the infinite
reaches of his mind. Stars whistle there
in the vacuum; shadow fades
into shadow, and he is falling —

he is disappearing into himself.
He peers into the well without bottom,
feels compelled to drink the black water,
slake his thirst in the liquid
that stands among the stars holding his eyes.

He lies awake in the dark of night
lost in the reaches of his mind,
disappearing into himself, into the well
of shadow, falling, hearing the stars whistle
in the vacuum filled with the water that holds his eyes.

Water rises in his throat. He sees himself
drowning in the well, in the infinite
reaches of his mind. He hears himself whistle
among the stars, shadow fading
into shadow, fading and falling.

APEIROFOBIA
La paura dell'infinito

E' sveglio nel suo letto
nel profondo della notte, contempla gl'infiniti
confini della sua mente. Le stelle sibilano
nel vuoto; le ombre si perdono
nelle ombre, e lui piomba —

scompare nel suo io.
Fissa il pozzo senza fondo,
ed è spinto a bere l'acqua nera,
ad estinguere la sua sete con il liquido
che è tra le stelle che lo incantano.

E' sveglio nel buio della notte
immerso nei suoi pensieri,
perduto nel suo io, dentro un pozzo
di ombre, cade, sente il sibilo delle stelle
nel vuoto pieno d'acqua che lo ammalia.

L'acqua gli arriva alla gola. Si vede
annegare nel pozzo, negl' infiniti
confini della sua mente. Sente il suo fischio
tra le stelle, ombre che si perdono
nelle ombre, si perdono e svaniscono.

AELUROPHOBIA
The Fear of Cats

She cannot stand their eyes, the way they stare
at her across the room, those lazy oval
pupils and the sleepy lids, the noisy purr
that sounds like a muted roar to her, as though
they waited slyly for the perfect time to pounce,

yawning to show the diminutive scimitars
that are their fangs. They like to toy with their prey —
the way they stare across the room purring.
How can people pet them? She shudders to think
of the smooth, soft, sleek, dissembling fur

beneath her fingers, the little knives hidden
in their sheaths like diminutive scimitars, the roar
in the dissembling purr. And when they walk!
the tail like a lashing snake, the soundless paws,
the grinning mouth hiding those little fangs. . . .

How can people pet them? How can they touch
the dissembling fur, how can they stand the eyes
staring across the room with their oval pupils,
the yellow eyes, the eyes that know her soul
cringing in her breast, in its hollow place.

AELUROFOBIA
La paura dei gatti

Detesta i loro occhi, come la fissano
dall'altro lato della stanza, quelle pigre pupille ovali,
le palpebre sonnolenti, le fusa rumorose
che le sembrano un ruggito smorzato, come se
aspettassero astutamente l'occasione per saltarle addosso,

sbadigliando per mostrare le loro zanne simili a piccole
scimitarre. Gli piace giocare con la loro preda —
come l'osservano dall'altro lato della stanza mentre fanno le fusa.
Come si fa a coccolarli? Rabbrividisce al pensiero del
liscio, soffice, morbido pelo che camuffa

sotto le unghia, i piccoli coltelli nascosti
nelle guaine come piccole scimitarre, il ruggito
delle fusa simulate. Che dire del loro felinare!
la coda come un serpente sferzante, le zampe silenziose,
la bocca sogghignante che nasconde quelle piccole zanne. . . .

Come si fa a coccolarli? Come si può toccare
il pelo che camuffa, come si fa a sopportare gli occhi
che la guardano dall'altro lato con le pupille ovali,
quegli occhi gialli, gli occhi che conoscono la sua anima
che si rannicchia nella cavità del suo seno.

PAPYROPHOBIA
The Fear of Paper

It stares back at him, a blank white sheet
of winter lying on his desk. They hypnotize
each other. He shakes his head and blinks his eyes,
takes up a pen and puts its nib upon
a random spot. He stops and stares some more,

lifts the pen and looks — a single dot
of darkness blooms like an iris off the slope
of winter. It does not help . . . it makes it worse.
He takes the sheet in his fist and crumples it,
throws it to the floor. He shakes his head

and takes another leaf out of the drawer,
takes up the pen and puts it down, leans back.
A field of frost lies waiting on his desk.
He feels its chill blooming off the slope
of his escritoire. When he shuts his eyes,

there it is again, blooming now
behind his irises, hypnotizing him
with sheets of winter desolation turning
slowly into dots of darkness spreading
downward from the alpine pinnacles.

PAPIROFOBIA
La paura della carta

E' fissato da un vuoto foglio bianco
d'inverno posato sulla sua scrivania. S'ipnotizzano
a vicenda. Lui scuote la testa e strizza gli occhi,
prende una penna e la punta
a caso sul foglio. Si ferma e continua a fissare,

alza la penna e guarda — un singolo punto
nero spicca come un'iris sul pendio
d'inverno. Così non va . . . anzi è peggio.
Prende il foglio nel pugno e l' accartoccia,
lo butta sul pavimento. Scuote la testa

e prende un altro foglio dal tiretto,
prende la penna e la lascia, si rilassa.
Un campo di ghiaccio l'aspetta sulla scrivania.
Sente il freddo emanante dal suo
scrittoio. Appena lui chiude gli occhi,

eccolo ancora, che appare
dietro le sue iridi, e l'ipnotizza
con fogli di desolazione invernale e si tramuta
lentamente in punti neri che scendono
allargandosi dalle vette alpine.

ERATOPHOBIA
The Fear of Poetry

Dear Cousin, she wrote, Thanks
for the books of poems. I must admit
that I haven't opened them. It's a source
of pride to me to have a poet in the family,
but I'm afraid I won't understand

the poems and I'd feel stupid.
I fear I haven't opened them.
I must admit I fear what lies in wait
between the covers: words that writhe,
that hiss at me off the page,

words that wriggle and won't hold still
to let me understand them.
Weird, huh? I'll work at it. I'll work
to get beneath the covers, to open one
in bed beneath the covers — they lie in wait

beside me on the nightstand. I'll reach out
one night and grab one, pull it underneath
the covers of my bed and, with a flashlight,
open it and see the poems writhing,
hissing at me on the page I fear.

ERATOFOBIA
La paura della poesia

Caro cugino, lei scrisse, grazie
dei libri di poesie. Devo confessare
che non li ho ancora aperti. E' un motivo
d'orgoglio avere un poeta in famiglia,
ma ho paura che non capisca

le poesie e mi sentirò stupida.
Mi dispiace ma non li ho aperti.
Devo ammettere che ho paura di quel che si
nasconde tra le copertine: parole che spasimano,
e sibilano dalle pagine,

parole che si dimenano irrequiete
e non si fanno capire.
Strano, eh? ci proverò. Farò in modo
di entrare sotto la copertina, ne aprirò uno
nel letto sotto la coperta — esse sono lì

ad aspettarmi sul tavolino accanto. Qualche notte
allungherò la mano e ne afferrerò uno, lo tirerò
da sotto la coperta del mio letto e, con una pila,
l'aprirò e vedrò le poesie spasimanti,
sibilanti dalla pagina che mi spaventa.

ENNUIOPHOBIA
The Fear of Boredom

He starts to worry. The job is almost done.
Is anything lined up? He looks ahead
even as he's concentrating on
the work in hand. The weekend's coming up.
His family will want him to do some things

with them: his wife will want to shop, the kids
will pull him around while she goes into stores
to try on this or that. He starts to worry,
tries to concentrate upon the work
he has in hand, but the weekend's coming up.

"T.G.I.F." somebody calls. He laughs, says "Yeah,"
but doesn't mean it. He looks ahead and sees,
with a touch of panic, two days of empty time
filled with nothing to do except putter
around the house, cut the grass, trim the hedge,

play with the kids while all this work goes begging —
how can he beg off? Can he bring some home?
His worry concentrates itself and he notices
he's not enjoying the work he's doing now,
still doing, the work in hand.

ENNUIOFOBIA
La paura della noia

Incomincia a preoccuparsi. Il lavoro è quasi finito.
C'è altro da fare? Guarda al futuro
anche quando si concentra sul
lavoro che ha tra le mani. Il fine-settimana si sta avvicinando.
La famiglia lo vorrà a casa per fare alcune cose

insieme: sua moglie vorrà andare a fare le spese, i figli
lo tireranno di qua e di là mentre la madre entra nei negozi
per provare questo o quello. Incomincia a preoccuparsi,
cerca di concentrarsi sul lavoro
che ha tra le mani, ma il fine-settimana si sta avvicinando.

"Meno male è venerdì." Qualcuno grida. Lui ride, dice "Sì,"
ma non vuol dir questo. Guarda al futuro e vede,
con un tocco di panico, due giorni sprecati
senza nulla da fare tranne che gingillarsi
intorno alla casa, mietere l'erba, potare la siepe,

giocare con i figli, mentre tutto questo lavoro rimane incompleto —
come può liberarsene? Può portarne parte a casa?
La sua preoccupazione aumenta e si rende conto
che non prova piacere nel lavoro che sta facendo ora,
ma continua a fare, il lavoro che ha tra le mani.

AMATHOPHOBIA
The Fear of Dust

If she closes her eyes, before she can drop
off the edge of silence into sleep
she imagines the dust beneath her bed
clumping itself, sending out strands of hair
to gather more dust, become a ball of fuzz,

and then begin to search for other balls of dust
with which to copulate and reproduce.
If it is a daylight nap she tries to steal,
her eyes spring open to see the noontide sun
slipping through the blinds in laddered beams

down which the motes of dust climb one by one —
she feels them landing on her chest, her face,
she feels them searching underneath her bed
to be caught in strands of hair, become a ball
of fuzz. She sneezes. She coughs. She begins to wheeze.

She throws off her coverlet to rise,
cover her mouth, walk to the kitchen through
the laddered beams of light and dust to find
the mop, the rag, the vacuum cleaner she
put away before she lay down to nap.

AMATOFOBIA
La paura della polvere

Se chiude gli occhi, prima di cadere
dall'orlo del silenzio nel sonno,
immagina la polvere che si accumula sotto
il letto, manda ciocche di capelli
per raccogliere altra polvere, formano un bioccolo di peluria,

poi va alla ricerca di altri bioccoli di peluria
con cui accoppiarsi e riprodursi.
Se cerca di rubare un pisolino in pieno giorno,
gli occhi spalancati per vedere il sole di mezzogiono
che filtra tra le persiane in una gradinata di raggi

che i granellini di polvere salgono uno alla volta —
li sente posare sul petto, sul viso,
li sente frugare sotto il letto dove
sono catturati da altre ciocche di capelli, diventano un bioccolo
di peluria. Starnutisce. Tossisce. Incomincia ad ansimare.

Si libera del copriletto e si alza,
si copre la bocca, va in cucina tra
la gradinata di raggi di luce e polvere per cercare
la scopa, lo straccio, l'aspirapolvere
che aveva messo a posto prima di farsi un pisolino.

MELANCHOPHOBIA
The Fear of Depression

He feels it first in his belly: a dying fall,
a slide and a lurching stop
at the brink of a pit that has opened in his mind.
He begins to whistle, then quits — that does no good;
breathes deep ten times. He hyperventilates:

oxygen saturates his blood, makes him dizzy,
nearly — lightheaded. He believes he's beaten it
and sighs with relief. Ten minutes later,
there it is again, the worm of despond
gnawing at his bowels, the dying fall,

the skid and lurching stop,
psychic heels dug in, at the brink
of the sinkhole of causeless sorrow.
He tries to read — that makes it worse. Music
seems to help a while, and then he turns

to television: the flittering images
ghost across the glass — he sees them through
a veil of descending mist. He goes out to run
the streets of his neighborhood, to slide and lurch
over the curbs and cobbles of his dread.

MELANCOFOBIA
La paura della depressione

Prima la sente nello stomaco: un tonfo mortale,
uno scivolone ed una fermata violenta
sull'orlo di un precipizio che si è aperto nella sua mente.
Comincia a fischiettare, poi si ferma — non ne vale la pena;
respira profondamente dieci volte. Rantola:

l'ossigeno satura il sangue, gli dà il capogiro,
quasi — lo manda in delirio. Pensa di averla superata
e dà un sospiro di sollievo. Dieci minuti dopo,
eccola di nuovo, il verme della disperazione
che rode le sue viscere, il tonfo mortale,

lo scivolone e la fermata violenta,
spiriti psichici sono affondati, sull'orlo
della foiba di un dolore senza causa.
Prova a leggere — è peggio. La musica
sembra di aiutarlo un pò, poi accende

la televisione: le immagini ondeggianti
zebrano lo schermo — le vede attraverso
un velo di nebbia che sta calando. Esce fuori per
vivere sulle strade del suo quartiere, per scivolare e barcollare
sui margini e sui ciottoli della sua fobia.

SABBATIPHOBIA
The Fear of Holidays

The calendar is her nemesis. The days drip off
the edge of the month bringing the holidays closer,
closer, ever so much closer. The pots and pans
that hang from pegs on the kitchen wall reflect
her dread, her consternation in shining copper

and stainless steel. Goodwill and jollity approach,
family values, thoughtfulness — she begins to suffocate
in the sea of expectations. The days drip off
her nemesis the calendar, begin to form a tide
of time that washes against the kitchen walls,

begins to rise to knees, to breast, to chin. She gasps.
So many things to do, shopping for gifts, for the tree,
for ornaments, baking, decorating,
sending the tastefully selected cards, displaying those
the mailman brings as the holidays come closer,

closer, ever so much closer. She can hardly breathe.
She loathes the calendar, her nemesis, the days that drip
off the edge of the month onto her kitchen floor,
turning the copper bottoms of her pans on the walls
a sickening green she remembers from childhood dreams.

SABBATIFOBIA
La paura delle feste

Il calendario è la sua nemesi. I giorni sgocciolano
dalla fine del mese, portando le feste più vicine,
più vicine, sempre più vicine. Le pentole ed i tegami
che pendono dagli uncini sulla parete della cucina riflettono
il suo terrore, la sua costernazione sul rame lucido

e sul metallo splendente. Si avvicinano amore ed allegria,
valori di famiglia, premura — comincia a soffocare
nel mare di attese. I giorni sgocciolano dal calendario
la sua nemesi, cominciano a formare una marea
di tempo che si abbatte sulle pareti della cucina,

comincia a salire fino alle ginocchia, al petto, al mento. Boccheggia.
Tante cose da fare, comprare i regali, l'albero,
gli ornamenti, fare dolciumi, decorare,
spedire le cartoline scelte con gusto, esibire quelle
che il postino consegna mentre le feste sono più vicine,

più vicine, sempre più vicine. Respira a fatica.
Detesta il calendario, la sua nemesi, i giorni che sgocciolano
dalla fine del mese sul pavimento della cucina,
coprendo il fondo di rame delle pentole sulla parete
di un verde nauseante che ricorda dai sogni d'infanzia.

PHALACROPHOBIA
The Fear of Balding

He washes his hair carefully in the shower,
massaging his scalp as gently as he can,
lathering twice, then working in conditioner,
rinsing at last. He sees it there afterward,
lying in the bottom of the tub —

a single strand of anguish, a filament
of rue. He picks it up and looks at it
accusingly. He turns the water off
and reaches for a towel. He dries himself
carefully, massaging his scalp as lightly

as he can. He looks into the mirror
over the sink and sees what he despairs
to see: the youngish man whose hairline even
in steam recedes almost from day to day,
whose eyes are wide with anguish and with rue.

He's washed his hair as carefully as he can,
lathering gently twice, rinsing at last
as though the man were father to the boy
he sees disappearing in steam and dream,
strand by strand, day by rueful day.

FALACROFOBIA
La paura della calvizie

Si lava accuratamente i capelli nella doccia,
massaggia gentilmente il cuoio capelluto,
insapona i capelli due volte, vi applica il balsamo,
e li risciacqua. Dopo li vede là,
 nel fondo della vasca —

un singolo filo d'angoscia, un filamento
di sgomento. Li prende e li osserva
con occhio accusatore. Chiude l'acqua
e prende un asciugamano. Si asciuga
con cura, massaggia gentilmente il cuoio

capelluto. Si guarda allo specchio
sopra il lavandino e vede ciò che ha paura
di vedere: il giovincello la cui capigliatura anche
bagnata si assottiglia quasi di giorno in giorno,
con gli occhi spalancati di angoscia e di sgomento.

Si è lavati i capelli con la massima cura,
insaponandoli gentilmente due volte, risciacquandoli alla fine
come se l'uomo fosse il padre del ragazzo che
vede scomparire in vapore e sogno,
un capello dopo l'altro, un giorno doloroso dopo l'altro.

ONEIROPHOBIA
The Fear of Dreams

Her eyelids will not close. She stares awake
into the darkness lying upon her chest,
pressing upon her face — she feels the night
breathing beside her in the double bed.
Although she cannot see them, still she knows

the images lurk among the shapes of the room,
waiting their chance to enter through her ears,
to insinuate themselves into her mind
through the apertures of her nostrils, of her mouth,
her eyelids that will not close. She stares, aware

of the images in the darkness, of the darkness,
creatures of shadow lying upon her chest,
pressing upon her face, breathing her breath,
absorbing her life like fear into their own
insubstantial masses.

They bide their time, those creatures of the night,
those images of shadow, they wait their turn
to enter her mind and begin their naked dance
in the starlit berth of nightfall lying behind
her eyes and the lifeline of her constricted breath.

ONEIROFOBIA
La paura dei sogni

Le palpebre non le si chiudono. Sveglia, fissa lo sguardo
nell'oscurità che le copre il petto,
le preme il viso — sente la notte
respirare accanto a lei nel letto a due piazze.
Benchè non le possa vedere, sa tuttavia che

le immagini si nascondono tra le ombre della camera,
aspettando l'occasione di entrare per le orecchie,
per penetrare nella sua mente
attraverso le narici, la bocca,
le palpebre che non le si chiudono. Fissa lo sguardo, cosciente

delle immagini nell'oscurità, dell'oscurità,
creature di ombra che giacciono sul petto,
premono sul viso, respirano il suo alito,
assorbono la sua vita come paura nella loro
stessa massa incorporea.

Aspettano l' occasione, quelle creature della notte,
quelle immagini dell'ombra, aspettano il loro turno
per entrare nella sua mente e cominciare la loro nuda danza
nel letto illuminato dalle stelle del crepuscolo che giace dietro
gli occhi ed il filo del suo alito compresso.

CHRONOPHOBIA
The Fear of Time

He hears his timepiece ticking in the night
beside the bed. Down the shadowed hall
each ponderous hour is rung by the standing clock.
He jerks awake and wonders why he has
these instruments of torment in his home.

He lies awake and hears the sandgrains fall
between the walls. The deathwatch beetle marks
behind his bed the moments of his life —
will daylight never dawn? Is all the world
forever lost in labyrinthine gloom?

He comes awake, rises and leaves his room
to wander down the hall. He hears the hour
rung by the standing clock. Its pendulum
swings through the moon, describing a silver arc
sixty times a minute — he hears the chatter

as though the sounds were rising from his brain.
Is all the world forever lost in sand
falling between the walls, deserts composed
of the moments of his life? He returns to bed
and hears his timepiece ticking in the night.

CRONOFOBIA
La paura del tempo

Ascolta nella notte il ticchettio dell'orologio
accanto al letto. Nel corridoio buio
ogni ora ponderosa è scandita dall'orologio a pendolo.
Si sveglia di scatto e si meraviglia di aver
in casa questi strumenti di tortura.

Giace sveglio e sente i granelli di sabbia cadere
tra le pareti. L'anobio annota
dietro il letto gli attimi della sua vita —
spunterà mai la luce del giorno? E' il mondo intero
smarrito per sempre in una labirintica malinconia?

Si sveglia, si alza ed esce dalla stanza
per vagare nel corridoio. Sente l'ora
scandita dall'orologio. Il pendolo
oscilla tra la luna, tracciando un arco d'argento
sessanta volte al minuto — sente il tintinnio

come se i suoni emanassero dal suo cervello.
E' il mondo intero smarrito per sempre nella sabbia
che cade tra le pareti, deserti formati
dagli attimi della sua vita? Ritorna a letto
e sente il ticchettio dell'orologio nella notte.

CATOPTROPHOBIA
The Fear of Mirrors

If she looks into the mirror she will see
no one she knows. The image there,
standing in a room of roses on the wall,
will be a stranger's; it will wear
the eyes of an assassin, the face

of the treacherous unknown. A wrinkle here,
a freckle on the cheek or near the nostril
might appear familiar — she does not dare
to turn about, confront no one she knows
standing in a sheet of wintry glass. The mere

of memory, the tarn that must accept
those cataracts of time, darken there
among the fading roses of the walls.
She does not dare turn and approach the mirror,
for she will meet a stranger, in the hall

of receding years, smoothing familiar hair
grown wintry among the roses on the wall.
The image will be a stranger's. She will stare
into those treacherous eyes and begin to drown
in the gaze of glass, in the tarn of memory there.

CATOPTROFOBIA
La paura degli specchi

Se si guarda allo specchio non vedrà
nessuna che lei conosca. La figura là
in piedi in una stanza di rose sulle pareti,
sarà di un'estranea; ostenterà
gli occhi di un assassino, il viso

della perfida sconosciuta. Una ruga qui,
una lentiggine sulla guancia o vicino alla narice
potrebbe sembrare famigliare — non osa
girarsi, confrontare chi non conosce
là in piedi in una lastra di vetro gelido. Lo stagno

della memoria, il laghetto che deve accettare
quelle cascate di tempo, s'intorbidisce là
tra le rose consunte delle pareti.
Non osa girarsi ed avvicinarsi allo specchio,
perchè incontrerà un'estranea, nel corridoio

degli anni sfuggenti, la consueta capigliatura liscia
invecchiata tra le rose sulla parete.
L'immagine sarà di un'estranea. Fisserà
quegli occhi perfidi e comincerà a naufragare
nello sguardo vitreo, là nel laghetto della memoria.

MNEMOPHOBIA
The Fear of Memory

He's walked these halls for nearly thirty years:
they used to house the school his kids attended,
now they hold his office. How has he stopped
thinking of picking them up in the afternoons
from the lot he parks in all day now?

Has he mislaid those memories? He recalls
seeing his daughter run down the corridor
toward him walking up the passage; his son
stopped in traffic to scoot a car along
the wall outside his office. How can it be

he never thinks of these when he comes to work?
And with the question come recollections borne
upon a tide of loss; waves of pain
wash down the halls. He nearly drowns in them.
His stomach fills and turns as his daughter jumps

into his arms — he pushes her aside,
blocks out his son, stops to raise the dikes
that kept him safe. He retches for air, then walks
again down the familiar corridor
where pools of memory eddy in every door.

MNEMOFOBIA
La paura della memoria

Ha vagato tra queste mura per quasi trent'anni:
una volta c'era la scuola frequentata dai suoi figli
ora c'è il suo ufficio. Perchè ha smesso
di pensare di prelevarli nel pomeriggio
dal posto dove ora parcheggia per l'intera giornata?

Ha dimenticato quelle rimembranze? Ricorda
che sua figlia gli correva incontro nel corridoio
quando lo vedeva entrare; suo figlio
si fermava nel traffico per lanciare una macchinetta lungo
il muro esterno del suo ufficio. Perchè

non pensa mai a questo quando viene a lavorare?
E con la domanda ritornano le reminiscenze nate
su una marea di dimenticanza . . .; ondate di dolore
lavano con forza i corridoi. Quasi vi annega.
Lo stomaco si riempie e si rivolta mentre la figlia gli salta

sulle braccia — la spinge da un lato,
blocca suo figlio, smette di sollevare gli argini
che lo mantennero al sicuro. Riprende fiato, poi s'incammina
di nuovo per il solito corridoio
dove cumuli di memorie turbinano ad ogni porta.

NEBULAPHOBIA
The Fear of Fog

The fog is rising . . . but not like Lazarus,
she hopes and prays, nothing like Lazarus —
more like the head of a fungus
rising to top out a summer morning.
She knows there's no reason to go into mourning,

none at all. So why is it she's in mourning
over the risen sun set on adorning
a mushroom here and there as the clouds disperse
across the blowsy sky, rush to disburse
scraps of storm across the universe? —

for now at least. There's a glamour in the air
and waterprisms whistling a liquid air
with eclat amounting to a flare
for causing one of a gloom-beridden cast
to lift her lids and seek the light at last.

Instead, she feels as though her livingroom
is full of webs of fog left over from
the morningful of summer morning gloom,
for the disappearing fog, like a slug or snail,
has touched the light and left a slimy trail.

NEBULAFOBIA
La paura della nebbia

La nebbia si sta alzando . . . ma non come Lazzaro,
lei spera e prega . . . non certamente come Lazzaro —
molto simile alla testa di un fungo
che affiora in un mattino estivo.
Si rende conto che non c'è motivo di affliggersi,

nessun affatto. Perchè dunque lei è triste
quando il sole appare ed adorna
funghi sparsi qua e là mentre le nuvole si disperdono
nel cielo rossastro, pronte a scaricare
qualche temporale nell'universo? —

almeno per adesso. C'è una magia nell'aria
e prismi d'acqua emanano goccioline
che brillano come fiamme che tremolano
capaci d'indurre una con il volto sconvolto
ad aprire gli occhi e cercare finalmente la luce.

Invece, le sembra che il salotto
sia pieno di lembi di nebbia lasciati indietro
dal grigio mattino estivo,
la nebbia che si dilegua, come un mollusco o una lumaca,
ha sfiorato la luce ed ha lasciato una striscia viscida.

AMNESIOPHOBIA
The Fear of Forgetting

For a moment he forgot to be afraid.
When he recalled his fear, his eyes
widened in disbelief. His hand
rose to touch the taut cords of his throat;
beneath the heel of his palm his heart

battered his chest. It was beginning —
he was beginning to forget himself,
his past, who he was and is. Whom will he be
should he forget? His eyes widened
in disbelief when he recalled his fear,

and he was afraid —
Beneath the heel of his palm his heart
battered his chest from within. How can he
be sure he is who he is now that he has forgotten
to be afraid? His eyes widen in wonder,

and he forgets again, forgets his fear
in disbelief, recalls it again. His hand
rises again to touch the cords of his throat
and he knows that he has killed the man he knew
to find the lethal stranger he must be.

AMNESIOFOBIA
La paura di dimenticare

Per un istante si dimenticò di aver paura.
Non appena se ne ricordò, gli occhi
increduli si spalancarono. Sollevò la mano
per toccare i muscoli irrigiditi del collo;
sotto la palma della mano il cuore

pulsava violentemente nel petto. Era l'inizio —
stava cominciando a dimenticare se stesso,
il suo passato, chi era, e chi è. Chi diventerebbe
se dovesse dimenticarsene? Gli occhi increduli si
spalancarono non appena si ricordò della sua paura,

e aveva paura —
sotto la palma della mano il cuore
pulsava violentemente dall'interno. Come può
essere sicuro di essere chi è ora che ha dimenticato
di aver paura? Gli occhi increduli si spalancarono di stupore,

e dimentica di nuovo, incredibilmente dimentica
la sua paura, la ricorda di nuovo. Solleva
di nuovo la mano per toccare i muscoli del collo
e s'accorge che ha ucciso l'uomo che conosceva
per trovare l'assassino sconosciuto che realmente è.

GERASCOPHOBIA
The Fear of Aging

Somewhere within these houses a woman looks
into a mirror and wonders why, or who
or when today has turned to mist and the sky
to leaves. Wherever else one looks a squirrel
seems to have a small request, but it

will still be weeks before the oaks manage
the feat of acorns. For now, the sun has gone
to earth, the trees brood in a pall of breathless
forenoon along the early summer streets,
among the late-arising neighbors. Here and there

a car coughs and begins to idle. The morning
papers materialize upon the verandas.
A schoolbus turns the corner saffron and then
disappears in a puff of smoke and gas.
In her room a woman wears a sapphire.

She looks into a mirror. Perhaps she lacks
that certain blue capacity, if she's lucky.
And if she's not, well, still she has the day,
the mist, the oaks, the squirrels, the mooning night
and the long dream of what is forever lost.

GERASCOFOBIA
La paura d'invecchiare

In qualche parte, tra queste case, una donna si guarda
allo specchio e si chiede perchè, o per chi,
o quando questa giornata si è trasformata in nebbia ed il cielo
in foglie. Dovunque si guardi, uno scoiattolo
sembra avanzare una modesta richiesta, ma

ci vorranno settimane prima che le querce porteranno
le ghiande. Per il momento, il sole è apparso,
gli alberi rimuginano nel manto di un mattino
senza vento per le strade all'inizio dell'estate,
tra i vicini tardi ad alzarsi. Qua e là

una macchina tossisce e comincia a ronzare. I giornali
del mattino appaiono sulle verande.
Un pulman scolastico di color zafferano svolta all'angolo e poi
scompare in una nuvola di fumo e di gas.
Nella sua camera una donna porta uno zaffiro.

Si guarda allo specchio. Forse non possiede
quella specie di qualità blu, se è fortunata.
E se non lo è, bè, ha ancora la giornata,
la nebbia, le querce, gli scoiattoli, la notte lunare
ed il lungo sogno di ciò che è perduto per sempre.

ARACHNOPHOBIA
The Fear of Spiders

He sees that the night is a dark web
and that the stars have come flying.
He hears the weasel sidling under the hill
where the long grasses are coarse.
The wind strikes a dim note, for the moon

is a dead eye beneath the stars struggling
over the hill where the owl ranges, the leaves
lie rustling in the coarse grasses. He hears
the wind as a dim note beneath the stars
trembling. On the hill a fox barks,

the spiders come floating upon the wind.
The blue stars lie quivering over the hill
as a weasel sidles through the grass. His fire
is a catamount hissing in the darkness
beneath the stars' keening. He hears the mole

listening to silence like a fog as the stars
come quaking, the weasel sidles under the hill.
The owl ranges the dead eye of the moon
while he sits at his fire listening for the spiders
floating in the blue wind, hissing in the darkness.

ARACNOFOBIA
La paura dei ragni

S'accorge che la notte è una ragnatela nera
e che le stelle sono arrivate in volo.
Sente la donnola che si muove furtivamente ai piedi della collina
tra le erbe alte e selvagge.
Il vento scocca una nota sorda, la luna

è un occhio spento sotto le stelle che spaziano
lentamente sulla collina dove il gufo erra, le foglie
frusciano tra le erbe selvagge. Sente
il vento come una nota sorda sotto le stelle
tremolanti. Sulla collina una volpe abbaia,

i ragni appaiono fluttuando nel vento.
Le stelle azzurre tremolano sulla collina
mentre una donnola si muove furtivamente nell'erba. Il suo fuoco
è un sibilo selvaggio nell'oscurità
sotto le stelle gementi. Sente la talpa che ascolta il

silenzio come la nebbia le stelle che si avvicinano
tremolanti, la donnola si muove furtivamente ai piedi della collina.
Il gufo esplora l'occhio spento della luna
mentre lui è seduto accanto al fuoco ascoltando i ragni
che fluttuano nel vento blu, che sibilano nell'oscurità.

ARITHMOPHOBIA
The Fear of Numbers

Onetwothreefourfivesixseveneightnineten
run through her brain tennineeightsevensixfive
fourthreetwoonenothing nothing nothing
can stop the drab cascade she goes to sleep
dreaming of numbers they indundate her dreams

and when she wakes the numbers on the clock
break upon her eyes she closes them
again and then the alarm goes off it shrieks
"It's six o'clock get up get up get up"
and so she does but in the shower the drops

cascade in avalanches down her body
in hundredsthousandsmillions a billion drops
too many to add they multiply divide
in rivulets of steam torrents of water
what can she do how can she escape

in numbers there is strength divide and conquer
sine and cosine no one can calculate
the drab cascades that multiply in her brain
waking or sleeping the terrifying ones
digits and tens fingers nose and toes.

ARITMOFOBIA
La paura dei numeri

Unoduetrequattrocinqueseisetteottonovedieci
scorrono nel suo cervello diecinoveottosetteseicinque
quattrotredueunozero niente niente
riesce a fermare la cascata monotona va a letto
sogna numeri che inondano i suoi sogni

e quando si sveglia i numeri sull'orologio
irrompono negli occhi li chiude
di nuovo e poi l'allarme suona stride
"Sono le sei alzati alzati alzati"
e così lei si alza ma nella doccia le gocce

precipitano sul corpo come una valanga
in centinaiamigliaiamilioni un miliardo di gocce
troppe da contare si moltiplicano si dividono
in rigagnoli di vapore torrenti di acqua
cosa può fare come può sfuggire

c'è forza nei numeri dividi e vinci
seni e coseni nessuno può calcolare
le cascate monotone che si moltiplicano nel cervello
sia quando è sveglio che quando dorme i numeri terrificanti
unità e decine dita naso e piedi.

AMBIVOPHOBIA
The Fear of Decisions

He will go to the valleys of Andorra; *He will stay*
in his brown room, the dark sunlight seeping
through the blinds. He will live in a cabin
on the lip of a gorge, listen in the chill wakening
to a river crying among the forests. *Tomorrow*

his eyes will open to the sounds of a thin child
calling news of war. The birds of the wood will weave
through clouds rising from the chimney.
The smell of labor will smother the city.
In the mountains of Andorra folk speak with the echoing

stone. *Listen — walls eat his voice. In the alleys*
old men cough. Death is visible
in the phlegm speckling the curb. He will go
to Andorra's valleys to live on a thin edge
which the blood hones and the bone grinds finely

as it moves beneath the skin. *He will stay*
in this brown room, on a bed snarled by night's
restless passage, hearing the Christmas bells
rattling upon the street corners, watching
the sunlight seep feebly through the blinds.

AMBIVOFOBIA
La paura di decidere

Se ne andrà nelle valli di Andorra; rimarrà
nella sua stanza marrone, mentre la luce pallida del sole trapelerà
attraverso le persiane. *Alloggerà in una capanna*
sull'orlo di un precipizio, ascoltando nella veglia fredda
un fiume che singhiozza tra i boschi. Domani

gli occhi si apriranno alla voce di un fanciullo gracile
che annuncia notizie di guerra. *Gli uccelli del bosco roteeranno*
tra le nuvole che si alzano dal camino.
Il fetore del lavoro soffocherà la città.
La gente parla con la roccia echeggiante sulle montagne

di Andorra. Ascolta — le pareti si mangiano la sua voce.
Gli anziani tossiscono nei vicoli. La morte è visibile
nel flemma che deturpa il marciapiede. *Andrà*
nelle valli di Andorra per vivere una vita spericolata
che il sangue che scorre sotto la pelle affila e

macina sottilmente le ossa. Rimarrà sul letto
in questa stanza marrone turbato dal passare
irrequieto della notte, ascolterà le campane natalizie
che echeggiano negli angoli delle strade, guarderà la
luce che penetra pigramente attraverso le persiane.

AMBIGUPHOBIA
The Fear of Puns

Neither hear nor dare to utter them:
that is her mutter as she walks the lane
between her home and work. No other theme
keeps her intention. Shakespeare is her bane
of contortion — all those double entendres,

wierd ploys, warble chokes. How can one stand
a language that sniggles like string, snags in the tongue?
A word should mean what it means and not demean
the person who speaks it, cause her demeanor to alter,
native good humor to melt in the foyer,

or before the altar, of the Laughing God.
She works the line between her ham and wok
when she pre-pares a meal. What is amiss? Better
to walk a mile than think of puns; sooner
choke on Oklahoma dust and walk a mule

than have as motto, "Neither hare nor deer
to otter dam." Better emigrate
to Rotterdam and get in Dutch
than stumble over meanings, double over,
wretched upon the quaking worth of words.

AMBIGUFOBIA
La paura del gioco di parole[1]

Nè sentirle, nè rischiare di proferirle:
è ciò che mormora mentre cammina per la strada
tra la casa ed il lavoro. Non c'è altro che
possa occupare la sua mente. Shakespeare è la causa
della sua angoscia — tutti quei doppi significati,

giochi di parole, scherzi di parole. Come si può tollerare
un linguaggio che vibra come una corda, s'impiglia sulla lingua?
Una parola dovrebbe significare ciò che significa e non degradare
la persona che la pronuncia, da alterarne il suo comportamento,
da dileguarne l'innato buon umore nel fuoco,

o davanti all'altare, del Dio Ridente.
Si divide tra casa e lavoro
quando prepara un pasto. Cos'è una signorina? E' preferibile
fare un miglio che pensare ai giochi di parole; piuttosto
soffocare nella polvere di Oklahoma e mettere un mulo al passo

che avere come motto, "Non proferirle nè qua
e nè là." Sarebbe meglio emigrare
a Rotterdam ed essere in difficoltà
che incespicare sui significati, rotolare,
infelice, sul valore vacillante delle parole.

---

[1]Nella traduzione si perde, purtroppo, l'effetto del gioco di parole.

ZELOPHOBIA
The Fear of Jealousy

Jealous beyond love or hate, he walks
past an armless Venus, helpless as
her marble passion. Down by the fountain, near
the wood, wild pigeons pitch and pander under
the leaves of the sycamore. With both hands

he scatters his crumbs of sorrow. They lie
upon the loam like lost thoughts until
the birds and squirrels, so like his fears,
partake of his personal disaster — or so
it seems, down by the fountain, near the wood

where, hour on hour he avoids the sun,
encounters merely sprinkles of light to work
together, if he can, into the whole
puzzle, filling in the dark and blind spots
with the dreams of wretched intellect. Upon

the harlot moss he lies at last and presses
his body down upon its sweet green flesh
to let his being wander past the fountain
into the wood beyond the armless Venus,
and be at one with love in her blue womb.

ZELOFOBIA
La paura della gelosia

Geloso oltre l'odio e l'amore, oltrepassa
una Venere monca, inerme come
la passione marmorea di lei. Giù alla fontana vicino
al bosco, colombacci si dondolano e tubano sotto
le foglie del sicomoro. Con entrambi le mani

disperde le briciole del suo cordoglio. Giacciono
sul terriccio come pensieri smarriti finchè
gli uccelli e gli scoiattoli, così simili alle sue paure,
condividono la sua calamità personale — o così
sembra, giù alla fontana, vicino al bosco

dove, per ore ed ore evita il sole,
s'imbatte in sprazzi di luce da intrecciare,
se può, nell'intero enigma,
riempiendo gli spazi neri e senza vita
con i sogni del misero intelletto. Finalmente

giace sul muschio seduttore e preme
il corpo sulla dolce e verde carne
permettendo al suo essere di vagare oltre la fontana
nel bosco oltre la Venere senza braccia,
ed essere uno con l'amore nel suo grembo blu.

MUNDANOPHOBIA
The Fear of the Ordinary

The maple across the street says something deeply
red; the one nearby, something green.
The speakers spill Mozart across the floor.
Along the walls the shelves of books attempt
to speak. The sun is taut between the limbs,

brittle upon the moving leaves. What's
to be done with such a day? What should one
be doing? How many days like this can anyone
count on? . . . That was yesterday. Today
rain spills across the trees like Gershwin.

The colors of the leaves trend to mist;
therefore, there is no boundary between
earth and sky, only a confusion of shifting
tones of gray settled over the city.
What a relief! One knows what one must do

on such a day — tend to business. If there were
no such things as mist, Mondays and rain
what would one look forward to? Chores
in the sun, the churning mower, softball in the park,
smoke rising through the sizzle of afternoon.

MUNDANOFOBIA
La paura dell'ordinario

L'acero dall'altro lato della strada mi suggerisce qualcosa
di profondamente rosso; quello vicino qualcosa di verde.
Gli altoparlanti diffondono Mozart sul pavimento.
Gli scaffali di libri lungo la parete cercano
di parlare. Il sole è diffuso tra i rami,

fragile sulle foglie moventi. Come
disporre di una tale giornata? Cosa
si dovrebbe fare? Quante giornate come questa
ci si può aspettare? . . . Quello era ieri. Oggi
la pioggia si spande tra gli alberi come Gershwin.

I colori delle foglie si fondono con la nebbia;
perciò non c'è linea di demarcazione tra
la terra e il cielo, soltanto una confusione di varie
tonalità di grigio è calata sulla città.
Che sollievo! Si sa ciò che si deve fare

in una giornata del genere — dedicarsi al lavoro. Se non ci fossero
tali cose come nebbia, lunedì e pioggia
cosa ci si potrebbe aspettare? Lavoretti domestici
nel sole, il rombo del tagliaerbe, softball nel parco,
fumo che si alza nel caldo torrido del pomeriggio.

ABOUT THE AUTHOR

LEWIS TURCO is a Distinguished Alumnus of the University of Connecticut from which he graduated in 1959. He took his M.A. from the University of Iowa in 1962, the same year in which he founded the Poetry Center of Cleveland at what he was then Fenn College, now Cleveland State University. He founded the Program in Writing Arts at S.U.N.Y. Oswego in 1968, directing it for the next 27 years and, in 1995, being the first faculty member ever to be designated Poet-in-Residence. He retired from teaching in 1996.

His first poems appeared in 1960, and the *Shifting Web: New and Selected Poems* in 1989. In 1968 he published *The Book of Forms: A Handbook of Poetics*, and its update, *The New Book of Forms*, in 1986, the same year in which he won the Melville Cane Award in literary criticism from The Poetry Society of America for *Visions and Revisions of American Poetry*. His most recent book, *Shaking the Family Tree, A Remembrance*, appeared in 1998 from Bordighera.

ABOUT THE TRANSLATOR

JOSEPH ALESSIA was born in Altomonte, Italy. He received his Teacher Certificate from G. Govone, Italy in 1956. He holds a Master of Arts from De Paul University, 1968; a Ph.D. from Indiana University, 1970. In 1983 he studied in Madrid, Spain where he completed a Master's Degree in Spanish language.

He has been a professor at Collegio San Leone Magno (Italy), 1956-63; a faculty member of the University of Colorado, 1968; Indiana University, 1968-70; Ohio State University, 1970-74; and S.U.N.Y. Oswego, 1974–, where he received a Chancellor's Award for Excellence in Teaching (1978); and where he is currently professor of Italian and Coordinator of Spanish, and director of the Italian summer program in Italy. He is the author of *Approfondiamo l'italiano* (1977) and *The Poetry of Dino Frescobaldi* (1983).